D0622442

Seasons of the
Desert
Biome

Written by
Shirley Duke

rourkeeducationalmedia.com

Scan for Related Titles
and Teacher Resources

www.rourkeeducationalmedia.com

PHOTO CREDITS: Cover: Patrick Poendl; Title Page © Anton Foltin; Page 4 © Anton Foltin and Mariusz Prusaczyk ; Page 5 © Laborant; Page 6 © Patricia Hofmeester; Page 7 © Volodymyr Goinyk; Page 8 © Cephas; Page 9 © RaJi and Christian Lopetz; Page 10 © Anton Foltin; Page 11 © BigWheel55 and Audrey Snider-Bell; Page 12 © Grobler du Preez; Page 13 © frangipani; Page 14 © Jerry Horbert; Page 15 © Tom Reichner and kangaroo rat courtesy of US Fish and Wildlife; Page 16 © Cat Downie; Page 17 © Janelle Lugge; Page 18 © Mila Gligoric; Page 19 © Lomvi2, staphy and globestock; Page 20 © Johnny Adolphson; Page 21 © AZP Worldwide and skodonnell

Edited by Jill Sherman
Cover design by Renee Brady
Interior design by Nicola Stratford bdpublishing.com

Library of Congress PCN Data

Seasons of the Desert Biome / Shirley Duke
(Biomes)
ISBN 978-1-62169-894-4 (hard cover)
ISBN 978-1-62169-789-3 (soft cover)
ISBN 978-1-62717-001-7 (e-Book)
Library of Congress Control Number: 2013936810

Also Available as:

Rourke Educational Media
Printed in the United States of America,
North Mankato, Minnesota

Rourke
Educational Media

rourkeeducationalmedia.com

customerservice@rourkeeducationalmedia.com • PO Box 643328 Vero Beach, Florida 32964

Table of Contents

Hot and Cold Deserts

What makes a desert? One thing sets deserts apart from other biomes. Deserts are dry. They get less than ten inches (25 centimeters) of rain a year.

Hot deserts have:
- Warm seasons
- Sand
- Little rain or precipitation
- Hardy plants

Cold deserts have:
- Cold seasons
- Icy and barren land
- Little rain or precipitation
- Hardy plants

Some of the rain never makes it to the ground. It **evaporates** into the dry air.

Some years have less rain than others. Some years may have no rain at all.

Shallow desert soil may be sandy or rocky.

Death Valley is located in California. It holds the record for the hottest place. On July 10, 1913, it was 134 degrees Fahrenheit (55.6 Celsius).

Not all deserts are hot. They can be cold, too. Snow falls instead of rain. But, most of the snow in cold deserts doesn't melt.

Antarctica is the largest cold desert. It holds the record for the coldest place. On July 21, 1983, it was -128.6 degrees Fahrenheit (-89.2 Celsius).

Hot Desert Seasons

Why are some deserts called hot deserts? You guessed it, most hot desert seasons are hot or warm. The Sun heats the land and dry air.

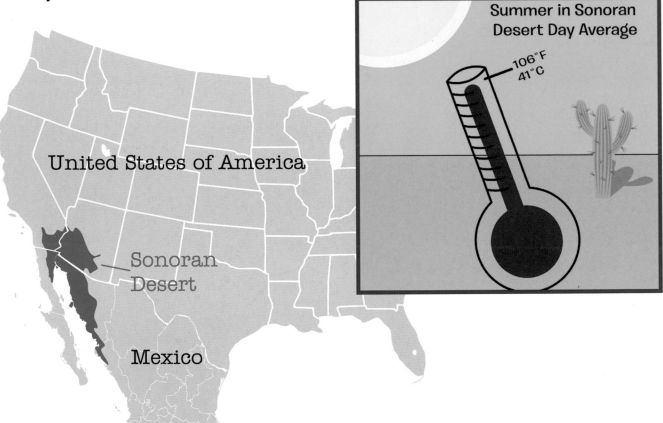

United States of America

Sonoran Desert

Mexico

Summer in Sonoran Desert Day Average

106°F
41°C

Temperatures in deserts at night cool down quickly because the air is so dry it doesn't hold in heat.

Summer in Sonoran Desert Night Average

77°F
24°C

In summer, the nights in Phoenix, Arizona, cool down almost 30 degrees.

When spring comes to the desert, flowers and **cacti** bloom.

Some animal young are born in dens. Bird eggs hatch in spring.

Cactus wrens mate for life and defend the territory around their nests.

Southern Pacific Rattlesnake

Snakes lay eggs in the sand. Rats and foxes make the desert their home. Birds, insects, and spiders live in hot deserts too.

Summer brings hotter days. Sometimes it rains in the summer.

In hot deserts, animals **burrow** to stay out of the heat. Others hunt during the cooler night. They sleep in daytime.

Ground Squirrel

Globemallow grows between rocks and desert washes. Poor soil and little water keep many desert plants like this one small in size.

Desert plants are suited for the dry, hot summer. Cacti stems make food and store water. Cacti have thin leaves called **spines** to protect them from being eaten by animals.

In the fall, the desert stays hot and dry.

Pear Cactus

No more rain falls. Plant growth slows.

Kangaroo rats get all their water from their food. They don't need to drink.

In the winter, deserts can get rain. Deserts make homes for many animals and plants. They have **adapted** to live there.

Desert Fox

Narrow bodies and large ears help keep animals cool. They don't need much water.

Dry desert air makes winter nights even cooler. **Reptiles** soak up the heat by day. Birds sit on cactus spines.

Thorny Devil Lizard

Cold Desert Seasons

20°F
-7°C

Even in the summer, cold deserts are still cold.

But not all deserts are hot and sandy. Cold deserts have just two seasons, winter and summer. Very few kinds of plants or animals can live in cold deserts. It is too dry and cold.

In cold deserts, animals and birds stay near the shore. Penguins, seals, and birds feed on sea life.

Penguins spend much of their time near the icy water feeding on fish, krill, and other small crustaceans.

Crabeater seals are curiously named since their major prey is not crabs but Antarctic krill.

Grasses and algae grow during the cold desert's summers.

Future of the Desert

People visit deserts to enjoy nature. They ride bikes or hike.

But people need roads and homes. They mine the land.

They **irrigate** and use water. Others leave trash. Animals lose their desert homes as people move in.

Plants brought by people replace **native** plants. Off-road drivers tear up the land. People must plan to save their deserts.

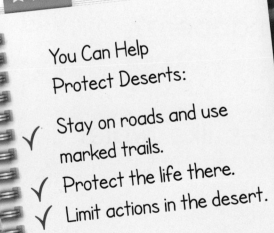

You Can Help Protect Deserts:

✓ Stay on roads and use marked trails.
✓ Protect the life there.
✓ Limit actions in the desert.

Irrigation removes what little water deserts have.

Study Like a Scientist
Disappearing Desert Water

1. Add water to a flat dish.

2. Mark the water line.

3. Put it in the sunshine.

4. Wait three days. What happens?

You got it! Water evaporates like water does in the desert.

Glossary

adapted (uh-DAPT-uhd): made a change to fit a different condition

burrow (BUR-oh): to dig a tunnel for a path or to live in under the ground

cacti (KAK-tye): more than one cactus, a spiny desert plant

evaporates (i-VAP-uh-rates): changes from a liquid, like water, to a gas in the air that can't be seen

irrigate (IR-uh-gate): to use pipes to bring water from another place to crops and plants

native (NAY-tiv): animals and plants that grow naturally in places

reptiles (REP-tiles): cold-blooded animal groups with short or no legs and scaly skin that lays eggs

spines (SPINZ): sharp, pointed growth on a plant like a cactus

Index

Websites

www.mbgnet.net/sets/desert/index.htm

kids.nceas.ucsb.edu/biomes/desert.html

www.neok12.com/Deserts.htm

About the Author

Shirley Duke has written many books about science. She lives in Texas and New Mexico and loves the different seasons in each place. She likes the Sonoran Desert and the saguaro and ocotillo cacti there. She's had jumping cholla cactus bounce up and hit her legs a few times, too.

Meet The Author!
www.meetREMauthors.com

24